That's Not a Pet!

CAN I HAVE A PET GORILLA?

By Bert Wilberforce

Gareth Stevens
PUBLISHING

Please visit our website, www.garethstevens.com. For a free color catalog of all our high-quality books, call toll free 1-800-542-2595 or fax 1-877-542-2596.

Library of Congress Cataloging-in-Publication Data

Names: Wilberforce, Bert, author.
Title: Can I have a pet gorilla? / Bert Wilberforce.
Description: New York : Gareth Stevens Publishing, [2019] | Series: That's not a pet! | Includes index.
Identifiers: LCCN 2017040517| ISBN 9781538217962 (library bound) | ISBN 9781538217986 (pbk.) | ISBN 9781538217993 (6 pack)
Subjects: LCSH: Gorilla–Juvenile literature. | Pets–Juvenile literature.
Classification: LCC QL737.P96 W55 2019 | DDC 599.884–dc23
LC record available at https://lccn.loc.gov/2017040517

First Edition

Published in 2019 by
Gareth Stevens Publishing
111 East 14th Street, Suite 349
New York, NY 10003

Editor: Therese Shea
Designer: Sarah Liddell

Photo credits: Cover, pp. 1, 21 Alan Tunnicliffe/Shutterstock.com; p. 5 Onyx9/Shutterstock.com; p. 7 bimserd/Shutterstock.com; pp. 9, 13, 24 (fruit) Kiki Dohmeier/Shutterstock.com; p. 11 lexan/Shutterstock.com; p. 15 David A. Northcott/Corbis Documentary/Getty Images; p. 17 Brina L. Bunt/Shutterstock.com; pp. 19, 24 (nest) Craig Melville/Shutterstock.com; p. 23 ullstein bild/Contributor/ullstein bild/Getty Images.

Printed in the United States of America

CPSIA compliance information: Batch #CS18GS: For further information contact Gareth Stevens, New York, New York at 1-800-542-2595.

Contents

I want a pet.
I want a gorilla!

Gorillas are
the biggest apes.
They live in Africa.

Their skin is black.
Their hair is mostly black.

They have long arms.
They walk on all fours
most of the time.

Gorillas live in forests.
They eat plants.
They love fruit.

They eat bugs, too.

Gorillas live
on the ground.
They climb trees, too.

They make nests
each day.
They sleep in them!

Gorillas are big
and strong.
They aren't good pets!

I'll see them at the zoo!

Words to Know

fruit

nest

Index